MW00512373

Copycat Recipes Making

The Easy Guide for Duplicating Your Favorite
Famous Fast Foods at Home

Danny Cook

Table of Contents

CHAPTER 1: BURGER RECIPES 9

  1. CARL'S JR. SIX DOLLAR BURGER...............................9
  2. HARDEE'S MUSHROOM SWISS BURGER 11
  3. CARL'S JR. WESTERN BACON CHEESEBURGER.........13
  4. IN-N-OUT DOUBLE-CHEESE BURGER 15
  5. A&W'S BACON CHEESEBURGER.............................17
  6. MCDONALD'S BIG MAC..19
  7. SONIC HICKORY BURGER 21
  8. GRIDDLE-SMASHED CLASSIC CHEESEBURGER........23
  9. KORZO'S BEET BURGER 25
  10. MCDONALD'S FILET–O–FISH SANDWICH 29
  11. APPLEBEE'S CLASSIC PATTY MELT 31
  12. MCDONALD'S HAMBURGERS...............................33
  13. A&W'S PAPA BURGER 35
  14. BURGER KING'S DOUBLE WHOPPER WITH CHEESE....37
  15. SHAKE SHACK'S BURGER 39
  16. FIVE GUYS BURGER...43
  17. MCDONALD'S EGG WHITE DELIGHT 45

CHAPTER 2: FRIES AND NACHOS RECIPES.................47

  1. BURGER KING COPYCAT CHICKEN FRIES 47
  2. CHILI'S TORTILLA CRUNCH CHICKEN FINGERS........49
  3. DON PABLO'S CHICKEN NACHOS 51

CHAPTER 3: SWEETS, COOKIES, AND ICE-CREAMS RECIPES 53

  1. DAIRY QUEEN ICE CREAM 53
  2. NUTTER BUTTER COOKIES...................................55
  3. EL TORITO'S DEEP–FRIED ICE CREAM 57
  4. O' HENRY BARS 59
  5. MCDONALD'S HOT APPLE & CHERRY PIE 61

CHAPTER 4: OTHER SNACKS RECIPES..........................63

  1. K.F.C. CRISPY STRIPS...63
  2. K.F.C. TWISTER 65
  3. LONG JOHN SILVER'S BEER-BATTERED FISH 66
  4. SONIC FRITOS CHILI CHEESE WRAPS....................69
  5. PANERA BREAD CAFE'S SIERRA TURKEY SANDWICH....71
  6. K.F.C.'S MAC AND CHEESE 73
  7. CHICK FILLET CHICKEN NUGGETS 75
  8. HOOTER'S BUFFALO CHICKEN WINGS 77

9. P.F. Chang's Lettuce Wraps 79

10. Ruby Tuesday's White Chicken Chili 83

CHAPTER 5: SAUCES, SLAWS, AND DIPS RECIPES **85**

1. A&W Coney Island Sauce 85

2. K.F.C. Pepper Mayonnaise Sauce 87

3. Long John Silver's Baja Sauce 88

4. K.F.C. Cole Slaw 89

5. Outback Steakhouse Bloomin' Onion Dipping Sauce 91

CHAPTER 6: BEVERAGES RECIPES **93**

1. Jack in the Box's Oreo Cookie Shake 93

2. McDonald's Mc Cafe Caramel Cappuccino 95

3. Starbucks Tazo Chai Tea Latte 97

4. McDonald's Oreo Mc Flurry 99

5. McDonald's Sweet Tea 101

6. Chili's Presidente Margarita 103

7. McDonald's Mc Cafe Peppermint Mocha 105

8. McDonald's Eggnog Shake 107

9. Colorado Bulldog Drink 109

CONCLUSION **111**

Introduction

I would like to thank and congratulate you for getting this book, Copycat Recipes.

People all over the world love to eat, enjoy and relax, especially in western countries. People love to go to restaurants to eat with their families, friends, and loved ones.

Whether you are a child or an adult, eating fast food outdoors has become a fast-growing trend. It is delicious and easy for everyone to enjoy. Many fast-food restaurants are opening all over the world due to the increasing demand of people.

Nowadays, hamburgers are people's go-to for fast food. If you live in America, you will know the value of burgers. It would not be wrong to say that America is the nation of burgers.

What if I told you that you can enjoy the famous fast-food dishes in the comfort of your own home?

Isn't that great?

Copied recipes truly inspire home cooking! Whether you are cooking for the whole family or entertaining with colleagues and friends. By following a copycat recipe, you will be able to serve an unforgettable meal that will bring joy to your family and friends.

This book mainly focuses on providing you with the replica recipes of the famous fast foods served all over the world by different fast-food restaurants.

Enjoy it!

Chapter 1: Burger Recipes

1. Carl's Jr. Six Dollar Burger

Preparation Time: 30 minutes

Servings: 1

Difficulty: Moderate

Ingredients:

- Half a pound of ground beef
- Salt and pepper, to taste
- One large sesame seed hamburger bun
- Three teaspoons mayonnaise

- Two teaspoons ketchup
- One teaspoon mustard
- 3–4 dill pickle slices
- One leaf of iceberg lettuce
- Two slices of tomatoes
- 4–5 red onion rings

Instructions:

1. Preheat the barbecue or indoor grill to medium heat.
2. Shape the ground beef into a large patty than the bun and add salt and pepper to either side of the patty.
3. On the grill, grill the burger for 3-4 minutes on either side or until cooked.
4. In a hot skillet over medium heat, brown the sides of the bun.
5. On the top and bottom of the buns, spread one and a half teaspoons of mayonnaise.
6. On the top of the bun, spread the ketchup and mustard.
7. Arrange the bottom of the bun with pickle slices.
8. On top of the pickles, add the lettuce, tomato, and onion.
9. Place on the bun the grilled burger and finish with cheese.

2. Hardee's Mushroom Swiss Burger

Preparation Time: 40 minutes

Servings: 4

Difficulty: Moderate

Ingredients:

- One (10.75-ounce) can of Campbell's Golden Mushroom soup
- One small can of sliced mushrooms
- One teaspoon of Worcestershire sauce
- Half teaspoon of Accent seasoning
- Half teaspoon of Lawry's Seasoned Salt
- a quarter teaspoon of ground pepper
- One pound of hamburger
- Four slices of Swiss cheese

Instructions:

1. Combine the mushroom broth, Worcestershire sauce and mushrooms.
2. Place the mixture over low heat in a small saucepan and let it boil.
3. Combine the hamburger with Accent, Seasoned Salt, and pepper.
4. Shape the hamburger into four patties and fry for 4-5 minutes per side in a skillet or grill until finished.
5. Place each patty on a bun and add the mushroom sauce and Swiss cheese.

3. Carl's Jr. Western Bacon Cheeseburger

Preparation Time: 50 minutes

Servings: 1

Difficulty: Moderate

Ingredients:

- Two frozen onion rings
- a quarter-pound of ground beef
- Two slices of bacon
- One sesame seed hamburger bun
- Two tablespoons barbecue sauce
- One slice of American cheese

Instructions:

1. According to box instructions, bake the onion rings.
2. Shape the hamburger into a patty and cook until cooked, for 4-5 minutes on either side.
3. Fry the bacon in a small skillet until crispy.
4. Toast the buns.
5. Spread the top and bottom of the bun with B.B.Q. Sauce.
6. Place the bottom of the bun on both onion rings.
7. Add the cooked hamburger, bacon, and cheese.

4. In-n-Out Double-Cheese Burger

Preparation Time: 30 minutes

Servings: 1

Difficulty: Moderate

Ingredients:

- One plain hamburger bun
- one-third pound of ground beef
- Two slices of American cheese
- One tablespoon of Thousand Island salad dressing
- One slice of fresh tomato
- One lettuce leaf
- One thin slice of onion

Instructions:

1. Preheat a barbecue or a frying pan. Toast both halves of the hamburger bun slightly and put them aside.
2. The beef is divided into two even portions and shape into patties. Use salt and pepper to season the patties. Cook per side for 4-5 minutes.
3. Place each hamburger patty on a slice of cheese and melt the cheese.
4. Assemble from bottom to top: bun, salad dressing, tomato, lettuce, burger, onion, burger, and bun top.

5. A&W's Bacon Cheeseburger

Preparation Time: 45 minutes

Servings: 1

Difficulty: Moderate

Ingredients:

- Three and a half ounces ground chuck
- Two teaspoons Kraft mayonnaise
- Salt and pepper
- Two Oscar Mayer ready-to-serve bacon slices
- Two teaspoons Kraft Original Barbecue Sauce
- One thin slice of tomato
- One slice of American cheese
- a quarter cup chopped iceberg lettuce
- One jumbo sesame seed hamburger bun, split in half
- Two Vlasic Ovals Hamburger Dill Chips

Instructions:

1. Just make the burger. Shape the ground chuck into a patty, 5 inches round and half an inch thick.
2. Place it on a piece of waxed paper, cover with another piece, and freeze for about one hour before cooking.
3. Combine the mayonnaise and barbecue sauce to create the secret sauce. Set aside.
4. Preheat an electric grill or light a grill with charcoal.

5. On the grill, put the partially frozen patty and cook 2 to 3 minutes per side until cooked through, then season with salt and pepper on both sides.

6. Microwave the bacon, until crisp, for 30 to 45 seconds. Drain on towels made of cloth.

7. When the split hamburger buns are grilled, put on the bottom half of the cooked burger and top with the tomato, bacon, cheese, lettuce, and pickles. On the top half of the bun, spread the secret sauce and cover the burger.

8. Wrap the sandwich in a sheet of 12 by 12 inches of foil and heat for 2 to 3 minutes in a 250 ° F oven, or wrap it in plastic and microwave for 10 seconds.

6. McDonald's Big Mac

Preparation Time: 40 minutes

Servings: 1

Difficulty: Moderate

Ingredients:

- One regular-sized sesame seed bun
- Two beef patties (2 ounces each flattened to bun size)
- Two teaspoons reconstituted onions
- One regular-sized plain bun
- Two tablespoons of Big Mac sauce
- One slice of real American cheese
- 1/4 cup shredded lettuce
- Two hamburger pickle slices

Instructions:

1. With the crown, discard half of the regular bun, preserving the heel. "Toast the heel and the "inner" sides of the sesame bun.
2. Much like standard burgers, the two-all-beef-patties must be prepared.
3. Lay one tablespoon of sauce on each of the heels while the bun elements are toasted. Then add 1/8 of a cup of chopped lettuce to each one.
4. Place one thin slice of American cheese on the bottom bun on top of the lettuce.

5. On the extra "heel," the middle bun, put the pickle slices on top of the lettuce.

6. Place them one at a time on both prepared buns when the meat patties are finished.

7. Stack the middle bun on top of the bottom bun and put the crown on top.

7. Sonic Hickory Burger

Preparation Time: 35 minutes

Servings: 1

Difficulty: Moderate

Ingredients:

- A quarter-pound of ground beef
- Salt and pepper, to taste
- One tablespoon of Barbecue Sauce
- One tablespoon of butter
- One tablespoon of chopped white onion
- One white hamburger bun
- one-third cup chopped lettuce

Instructions:

1. Preheat over medium heat, the skillet or a pan.
2. Form the shape of a patty from the grounded beef. Season it with salt and pepper. Melt the butter in the pan or skillet. Then toast the buns mildly to light brown. Suspend and leave aside.
3. In the same pan or skillet, grill the beef for 3–4 minutes on each side until cooked.
4. Your burger is made from the bottom by adding first the barbecue sauce, then onion, followed by lettuce, burger and top bun.

8. Griddle-Smashed Classic Cheeseburger

Preparation Time: 45 minutes

Servings: 8

Difficulty: Moderate

Ingredients:

- Eight potato buns
- Two pounds fresh-ground 80/20 chuck
- Peanut oil or other neutral oil
- American cheese, thinly sliced
- Salt, for seasoning

Instructions:

1. Toast the buns on a preheated flat top or in a preheated cast-iron skillet and set them aside.

2. Preheat over low heat (or a flat top to medium) the cast-iron skillet and apply a drop or two of peanut oil. To spread the oil, use the spatula, covering the cooking board.

3. Place the chuck on the field in a mixing tub. Using the salad scoop, make beef balls, and as you go, put them on the heated skillet. Each ball should have approximately 7 cm (3 inches) of space around it.

4. Sprinkle each beef ball with a generous pinch of salt and press them flat, firmly, with a stiff spatula. Each ball is squeezed until it's a wide patty, only a little smaller than the bun it's about

to hit.

5. Move back until the patties are smooth, and don't touch them again. Let them cook on the patties' surface for two and a half minutes or until the reddish liquid starts to form.

6. Flip them once and avoid the urge to push again on the patties.

7. Combine each patty with a slice of cheese and let them cook for another 2 minutes.

8. Take the burgers from the skillet and put them on the toasted white buns.

9. Korzo's Beet Burger

Preparation Time: 40 minutes
Servings: 8
Difficulty: Moderate
Ingredients:

- One large beet, peeled for roasting
- 30 ounces (850 grams) canned black-eyed peas, drained and rinsed
- Four cups (400 g) walnuts, soaked overnight in water and drained
- Two medium carrots, peeled and shredded in a food processor with a shredding attachment
- One large raw beet, peeled and shredded
- Two cloves fresh garlic, minced
- One tablespoon Korzo Ale Mustard (or any right, grainy mustard)
- Two tablespoons Frank's Red Hot cayenne pepper sauce or similar hot sauce
- One cup (80 g) panko bread crumbs
- Salt and black pepper, to taste
- Two tablespoons salted butter
- Eight soft half-wheat or sturdy soft burger rolls, toasted

Instructions:

1. Preheat the oven to 205 °C (400 °F). Use olive oil to rub the beet and cover it in two layers of aluminum foil. Roast for one and a half an hour, or before a knife quickly slips through the entire way. Let it cool, chop it into cubes, and set it aside. Reduce the temperature of the oven to 190°C (375°F).

2. The black-eyed peas are coarsely blended in a food processor and moved to a large mixing bowl. In the food processor, cut the walnuts until coarse and add them to the peas' mixing bowl.

3. In the same bowl, add the vegetables, all raw and roasted beets, garlic, mustard, hot sauce, and bread crumbs, and combine until combined by hand. Season with salt and pepper.

4. There should be a dense, pasty consistency of the mixture.

5. Shape patties with a thickness of about a quarter-inch (6 mm) (patties can be chilled and frozen for later use). During frying, these burgers will not compress, so shape patties that are near to the diameter of your buns.

6. Place the patties (or baking sheet with a silicone baking liner) on the non-stick baking sheet and roast for 45 minutes.

7. Prepare the sautéed mushrooms and caramelized onions as the beet burgers cook.

8. Remove them from the oven when the burgers are done baking. Over medium heat, preheat the cast-iron skillet and apply a pat of butter. Brown one of the patties on both sides, gently rotating the burgers, so they don't fall apart.

9. To the top of each burger, add a spoonful of sautéed mushrooms, preceded by a slice of cheese.

10. Cover and finish cooking for another 2 minutes before the cheese is melted.

11. Move the finished beet burgers and top with the caramelized onions to the toasted buns.

10. McDonald's Filet–O–Fish Sandwich

Preparation Time: 55 minutes

Servings: 1

Difficulty: Moderate

Ingredients:
- Two tablespoons mayonnaise
- Two teaspoons sweet relish
- Two teaspoons minced onion
- Two hamburger buns
- Two square breaded frozen fish portions
- Two slices of American cheese

Instructions:
1. In a shallow bowl, combine the mayonnaise, relish, and minced onion. It's going to be the tartar sauce.
2. Toast the hamburger buns gently.
3. Cook the fish according to the box instructions by either baking or frying it in oil.
4. Divide the tartar sauce, spread it uniformly on each of the top buns, and put each of the bottom buns a slice of cheese.
5. On each sandwich, put the fried fish on top of the cheese slice.
6. Place and serve top buns on the fish.

11. Applebee's Classic Patty Melt

Preparation Time: 45 minutes

Servings: 1

Difficulty: Moderate

Ingredients:

- One burger patty
- Two pieces of Italian bread
- Salt and pepper, to taste
- Granulated garlic, to taste
- Melted butter as needed

- Two slices of Cheddar cheese
- Two tablespoons of mayonnaise mixed with roasted garlic and mustard
- Two slices of Swiss cheese
- Half cup sliced onion

Instructions:

1. Season one side of the burger with salt, pepper, and garlic. Place in the broiler on a grill or, seasoned side down. After the other side is seasoned. Cook to the level of doneness required. When the burger is cooking, melt the butter in a frying pan over medium heat or an electric skillet (set at 350 degrees Celsius).

2. Spread on the toast, mayonnaise. Into melting pools, lower bread, dry side down, and swirl to coat (to avoid sticking). To coat one slice of bread and two slices of Cheddar on the other, use two slices of Swiss cheese.

3. In a separate frying pan, heat the butter and roast the sliced onions. Heat and add salt, pepper, and garlic to season. Place the fried burger patty on top of one cheese-topped bread slice and the sautéed onions on the other. Gently close the sandwich and split.

12. McDonald's Hamburgers

Preparation Time: 40 minutes

Servings: 10

Difficulty: Moderate

Ingredients:

- One pound ground chuck
- Ten teaspoons dried, chopped (not minced) onions
- Ten hamburger buns
- Mustard
- Ten hamburger dill slices
- Ketchup
- Salt, Pepper, and M.S.G.

Instructions:

1. Divide one pound of beef into ten balls of similar size. Shape a patty roughly 4 inches in diameter and a quarter-inch thick from each ball. On waxed parchment, do this. Freeze the patties for at least one hour. Combine the dried onions in a small tub of water. Apply enough water that you can hydrate the onions.

2. Preheat a medium to large griddle or skillet. Toast the hamburger buns until just crispy in the meantime.

3. On the hot table lie the frozen patties. After about 20 seconds, "sear" them with the back of a metal spatula by adding even pressure; do so for about 2 seconds only.

Sprinkle generously with salt, pepper, and M.S.G. to taste after searing them.

4. Switch them over after about one minute of searing the patties.

5. Take note, don't tear down the part you seared. Add on top around one teaspoon of your prepared onions.

6. Dress your buns easily. On top, mustard first, then the ketchup, five squirts the nickel's
size in the pattern found on dice.

7. Place the pickle in the middle.

8. The meat is done by the time you finish it (about 1 minute or 1:10 after turning).

9. To allow excess fat to drain off, remove the meat and tilt it to the side. To keep the onions down, use your free hand.

10. On the dressed crown, spot patties onion side up, top with toasted heels.

11. Upright flip and serve.

13. A&W's Papa Burger

Preparation Time: 45 minutes

Servings: 1

Difficulty: Moderate

Ingredients:

- Three and a half ounces ground chuck
- One tablespoon Kraft mayonnaise
- Two teaspoons hamburger relish
- Salt and pepper
- One jumbo sesame seed hamburger bun, split in half
- One slice of American cheese
- a quarter cup chopped iceberg lettuce
- Two classic Ovals Hamburger Dill Chips

Instructions:

1. First, build the burger. The ground chuck is first shaped into a patty, 5 inches round and half an inch thick. Place it on a waxed paper, cover with another slice, and freeze before cooking for 1 hour.
2. By mixing the mayonnaise and relish, create the Teen sauce. And set aside.
3. Preheat an electric grill or light a grill with charcoal.
4. On the grill, put the partially frozen patty and cook 2 to 3 minutes per side until cooked through, seasoning with salt and pepper on both sides.

5. Get the split hamburger bun grilled until toasted. Place the bottom half of the grilled burger and cover it with the cheese, lettuce, and pickles. On the top half of the bun, scatter the Teen Sauce and coat the burger.

6. Wrap the sandwich in a sheet of 12 by 12 inches of foil, cook for 2 to 3 minutes in a 250 ° F oven, or wrap it in plastic and microwave for 10 seconds.

14. Burger King's Double Whopper with Cheese

Preparation Time: 20 minutes

Servings: 1

Difficulty: Easy

Ingredients:

- Two quarter-pound of beef patties thinly pressed and round
- One sesame seed burger bun
- Two tablespoons butter
- Two tablespoons mayonnaise
- Two slices of tomato
- Dill pickle slices
- Two slices of Cheddar deli
- Chopped lettuce
- Onion slices
- Salt and pepper to taste
- Ketchup

Instructions:

1. Heat the gas or prepare the B.B.Q. until very hot. You want the coal to be white-hot if you use charcoal.
2. Start by getting your bun ready. Toast your buns, slice down your side in a little butter
   before they're browned perfectly.

3. On the top bun, layer the mayonnaise.

4. Now, on the hot grill, put your burger patties and cook for about two minutes. It should not take long for them to cook, since they are so thin.

5. With salt and pepper, season the burgers generously, and then turn them over.

6. Cover with the slices of cheese and grill for another few minutes.

7. Place one patty on top of the other when cooked to your liking, and shift to the bottom bun.

8. Cover the sliced pickles with the egg, accompanied by three ketchup rings.

9. Now put the onion rings, followed by the tomatoes (place side by side) and then the shredded lettuce on top of the ketchup.

15. Shake Shack's Burger

Preparation Time: 55 minutes

Servings: 8

Difficulty: Moderate

Ingredients:

For sauce

- Half cup mayonnaise
- One tablespoon ketchup
- One teaspoon pickle brine
- Pinch of paprika
- 1/4 teaspoon ground cayenne

For Buns

- Potato Rolls or White Hamburger Buns
- Two tablespoons unsalted butter melted

Meat

- Two pounds of ground beef
- Freshly ground pepper
- Sea salt

For cooking

- Vegetable oil
- Mustard
- Roma tomatoes cut into half-an-inch slices
- Eight slices of American cheese
- Sliced pickles

- Baked crinkle fries
- Leafy Green Lettuce
- Ketchup

Instructions:

Sauce

1. Put the special sauce ingredients into a bowl and whisk until smooth.
2. Move and set aside in a little bowl or squeeze bottle.
3. Buns
4. Use butter on the buns (top and bottom).
5. Over medium heat, warm a skillet. Add the buns when warmed, then toast them for around 1 to 2 minutes.
6. For all the buns, repeat it.

Meat

1. Divide the meat into mounds of 4 ounces.
2. Make the pucks that are around 2 inches high and 2 inches wide. Afterward, dust the
   top of the buns with salt and pepper.

Cooking

1. Over the medium-high fire, position a cast-iron skillet.
2. Add a few teaspoons of oil, then add a meat puck when it is glowing and very hot.
3. Enable about 30 seconds to cook and then break it until it's about 1/4-inch thick with a spatula.
4. Cook for about 1 minute, then apply to the top a couple of pinches of salt and pepper. Flip, then.

5. Add the cheese slice and cook for about an extra minute or so.

6. Remove from the mixing pan and replicate for the remaining meat pucks.

Assembly

1. On both sides of the bun, squeeze a bit of special sauce.

2. Add a pair of leafy green lettuces, a couple of tomato slices, and then top with the patty burger.

3. Add a few pickles, and the other half of the bun is added on top. Repeat until you have all the hamburgers made.

4. Serve with side-side fried crinkle fries, ketchup, and mustard.

16. Five Guys Burger

Preparation Time: 20 minutes

Servings: 4

Difficulty: Easy

Ingredients:

- One lb. ground beef
- One teaspoon garlic powder
- Salt and pepper, as desired
- Four slices of American cheese
- Hamburger buns

Instructions:

1. Preheat the griddle to a medium-high temperature on the stovetop.
2. In a small bowl, combine the ground beef, garlic powder, salt, and pepper.
3. Separate it into four wide balls.
4. Place each ball between 2 wax paper pieces.
5. Press the balls softly into smooth disks using the bottom of a shallow frying pan.
6. Put each patty of the hamburger on the hot griddle. For 2 to 3 minutes, cook. On the other hand, flip and repeat.
7. On top of each patty, arrange the sliced American cheese and allow it to melt.
8. Serve your favorite toppings on fluffy hamburger buns.

17. McDonald's Egg White Delight

Preparation Time: 45 minutes

Servings: 2

Difficulty: Moderate

Ingredients:

- Two wheat English Muffins
- Four egg whites
- Two slices Canadian Bacon
- Two slices of Cheddar cheese
- salt and pepper

Instructions:

1. Toast English muffins with wheat in a toaster.
2. Heat the Canadian bacon in a small skillet until hot and finely browned. Suspend the bacon from the skillet. Set the egg whites apart from the yolk and reserve the yolks for a later recipe.
3. Whisk all the egg whites together. Spray some non-stick spray for it.
4. Place the egg whites in the skillet and get the heat down to a low level.
5. Cook the egg whites slowly. If required, season with salt and pepper. Assemble the sandwiches after the egg whites have been fried.
6. Divide the white eggs into two pieces. Place the egg whites on the English muffins' rim.

7. To each of the egg muffins, add one slice of cheese.

8. Top with a Canadian bacon slice and the top bun.

Chapter 2: Fries and Nachos Recipes

1.Burger King Copycat Chicken Fries

Preparation Time: 60 minutes

Servings: 2

Difficulty: Easy

Ingredients:

- One package of boneless skinless chicken breasts
- Half cup of flour
- Half cup of Zatarain's Fish-Fri
- One egg
- One tablespoon water
- Vegetable oil for frying

Instructions:

1. Butterfly the chicken breast. Trim them down to the center to separate the breast halves. Slice them into the shape of French fries with meat scissors or a knife.
2. Then add the flour and Fish-Fri into two identical zip-top plastic bags.
3. In a little cup, beat the egg gently with the water.
4. Put four chicken fries at a time into the flour bag. Shake off the additional flour.

5. Dip them into the egg wash at Fish Fri, shake off the waste, then shake.

6. Place each chicken fry on a tray to reserve for frying.

7. In a medium-high skillet, heat the oil. Batch-fry, the chicken fries, rotating until they are golden brown (about 4-5 minutes or until they float)

8. Drain on paper towels.

2. Chili's Tortilla Crunch Chicken Fingers

Preparation Time: 2 hours 10 minutes

Servings: 6

Difficulty: Moderate

Ingredients:

- One package of dry onion soup mix
- One teaspoon crushed red pepper flakes
- Two tablespoons s butter or margarine, melted
- A quarter teaspoon of cayenne pepper
- 1/8 teaspoons ground cumin
- One and a half lb. boneless skinless chicken breasts
- One egg
- One C. crushed tortilla chips
- Two tablespoons water

Instructions:

1. Preheat the oven to 375°F. Use vegetable cooking spray to coat a large baking sheet. Combine a mixture of dry onion soup, red pepper flakes, cayenne pepper, cumin, and tortilla chips; set aside.

2. Whisk the egg and water together; set aside. Place the chicken breasts between two pieces of plastic wrap and lb, to a thickness of even 1/2-inch. Cut into strips that are 1/2 x 3-inch.

3. Dip strips into the egg and then into the mixture of tortilla chip/spice, coating well.

   Arrange on a prepared baking dish in a single layer; drizzle with butter.
4. Bake for 15 to 18 minutes uncovered, or until the chicken is done and the top is golden and crispy.

3.Don Pablo's Chicken Nachos

Preparation Time: 45 minutes

Servings: 2

Difficulty: Moderate

Ingredients:

- Ten large flat tortilla chips
- three-fourth cup shredded Cheddar cheese
- Half cup refried beans
- Half cup chopped cooked chicken
- Shredded lettuce
- One tablespoon sliced jalapeño pepper
- a quarter cup sour cream
- Three tablespoons diced tomatoes

Instructions:

1. On a warmed large serving platter, layer the chips and sprinkle with half of the Cheddar cheese. Spoon over the cheese with the warmed beans, then top with the cooked chicken and finish off with the remaining cheese.

2. On one side of the platter, place the lettuce and layer the jalapeño slices on top. With dollops of sour cream, garnish the nachos and finish with the diced tomatoes.

Chapter 3: Sweets, Cookies, and Ice-creams Recipes

1. Dairy Queen Ice Cream

Preparation Time: 2 hours 10 minutes

Servings: 12

Difficulty: Moderate

Ingredients:

- Two envelopes of Knox gelatin
- Half cup cold water
- Four cups whole milk
- Two cups of sugar
- Two teaspoons vanilla extract
- Half teaspoon salt
- Three cups cream

Instructions:

1. In cold water, soak Knox gelatin. Heat your milk, but don't boil it.
2. Remove it from the heat and add the gelatin, sugar, vanilla extract, and salt. Refrigerate it, and then add the ice cream. Afterward, for 5 to 6 hours, refrigerate and then savor.

3. Pour in a 4 to 6-quart freezer of ice cream. Then process it as per the instructions of the manufacturer.

2.Nutter Butter Cookies

Preparation Time: 40 minutes

Servings: 12

Difficulty: Moderate

Ingredients:

For Cookie

- Half cup vegetable shortening
- 2/3 cup granulated sugar
- One egg
- Half teaspoon salt
- Three tablespoons peanut butter (regular)
- Half cup old–fashioned Quaker oats
- One cup all–purpose flour

For Filling

- Half cup peanut butter
- 3/4 cup powdered sugar
- One tablespoon of fine graham cracker crumbs

Instructions:

1. To 325F, preheat the oven. Cream the shortening and sugar together with an electric mixer. Add the egg, peanut butter, and salt and beat until well combined.

2. Put the oats in a blender and mix until they are almost as finely ground as flour, at medium velocity.

3. To the mixture, add the oats and flour and blend well.

4. Roll the dough into 1-inch balls with your hands. Press them to flatten to form 2-inch circles on uncoiled cookie sheets.
5. Bake for 8 to 10 minutes, or until the sides are light brown.
6. In a small bowl, mix the filling ingredients as the cookies bake.
7. When the cookies are cold, spread a thin layer of filling on a cookie, place another one on top, and then serve.

3. El Torito's Deep–Fried Ice Cream

Preparation Time: 45 minutes

Servings: 12

Difficulty: Moderate

Ingredients:

- 20 ounces chocolate chip ice cream
- Two cups of 4–grain flake cereal, crushed
- One and a half tablespoons sugar
- Three and a half teaspoons ground cinnamon
- Two eggs
- One teaspoon water
- Four (8–inch) flour tortillas
- Oil for deep–frying
- Cinnamon mixed with sugar
- Whipped cream
- Four maraschino cherries

Instructions:

1. Shape the ice cream into four balls.
2. Place the mixture in the baking pan and freeze for 2 hours or more.
3. Combine the cereal, cinnamon, and sugar. Divide between 2 pie plates or other

   shallow containers in equal quantities. Eggs are beaten with water.

4. In a cereal mixture, roll each ice cream ball and press the coating into the ice cream.

5. Dip the coated ball in the egg wash, then roll it in the second cereal mixture container.

6. Press the coating on the ice cream again. Reliable Freeze Coated Ice Cream Balls, 4 to 6 hours.

7. Cut off a curved slice from 2 opposite sides, shape each tortilla into hourglass form (with a narrow waist). For ice cream, one end will act as the foundation. There'll be a decorative fan on the other end.

8. Heat a wok or broad deep-fryer with oil. Place the tortilla between 2 ladles of varying sizes or large spoons (smaller ladle on top).

9. With the back of the upper fan held by the handle of a larger spoon, position the tortilla such that the base end is cupped into the larger spoon to form a basket.

10. Deep-fry until squeaky. Drain and apply cinnamon-sugar to sprinkle. Only put aside.

11. For 30 to 45 seconds, deep-fry frozen coated ice cream balls. In a wide stemmed bottle, put
each fried tortilla, with the tortilla's fan portion standing vertically above the glass. Place a ball of fried ice cream on the base of the tortilla.

12. Place a dollop of whipped cream on top and garnish with a raspberry.

4. O' Henry Bars

Preparation Time: 35 minutes

Servings: 4 to 6

Difficulty: Moderate

Ingredients:

- 2/3 cup margarine
- One cup of brown sugar
- Half cup light corn syrup
- Three teaspoon vanilla
- Four cups instant oatmeal

Topping

- 6 oz. chocolate chips
- 2/3 cup peanut butter

Instructions:

1. Mix all the above ingredients.
2. Spread oil on a 13x9 baking tray. Bake at 350 degrees F or 15 minutes. Take it out and allow it to cool. Melt the chocolate chips and peanut butter in a saucepan.
3. Spread the mixture onto the cooled mixture of oatmeal and refrigerate until the topping of chocolate/peanut butter is firm, then slice and consume.

5. McDonald's Hot Apple & Cherry Pie

Preparation Time: 2 hours

Servings: 4 to 6

Difficulty: Moderate

Ingredients:

- 4–6 Cups vegetable oil (in the fryer)
- One package Pillsbury apple or cherry turnovers

Instructions:

1. For the Pillsbury turnover, unroll the dough. You are going to have six 3"x3." pieces. Make use of 4 of them.

2. Stretch them out into about 4'x5 rectangles.' Do this on waxed parchment.

3. On one dough and half of the other, scatter half of the pie filling, leaving about 1/2" of dough around the edges. Clear a 3/4" space down the middle of both.

4. Use the filler and place the remaining two on top of the two doughs. Make you crimp the corners. You're going to get what two major pop-tarts look like.

5. Cut both of them precisely down the center in the 3/4" space you made. Crimp the two edges."

6. Manipulate, as desired, to form an attractive, uniform shaped pie. They are supposed to look like tiny burritos, just around the edges, crimped.

7. Place all four of these, flat on waxed sheets, in the refrigerator. Spray the mist with water on both sides of each pie after about forty-five minutes. Send it to the fridge for at least an additional hour. Place them in a freezer bag and lock them or prepare them for deep frying for potential use.

Chapter 4: Other Snacks Recipes

1. K.F.C. Crispy Strips

Preparation Time: 40 minutes

Servings: 6

Difficulty: Moderate

Ingredients:

- Six chicken breasts
- Vegetable oil for frying
- One eg1 cup milk
- Two cups flour
- Two and a half teaspoons salt
- three-fourth teaspoon pepper
- 1/8 teaspoon garlic powder
- 1/8 teaspoon paprika
- 1/8 teaspoon baking powder

Instructions:

1. Slice the breasts of the chicken into strips.
2. Preheat the oil to 350°F in a skillet or deep fryer.
3. Beat the egg and the milk in a small bowl.
4. Combine the flour and spices in another bowl.
5. Dip the strips of chicken into the egg mixture one at a time. Then dip the flour coating into it.

6. Fry a few strips until they are golden brown at the same time. Cook for or before the strips float for about 5 minutes.

7. To extract excess oil, wipe on a paper towel.

2. K.F.C. Twister

Preparation Time: 45 minutes

Servings: 6

Difficulty: Moderate

Ingredients:

- One large flour tortilla
- K.F.C. Pepper Mayonnaise Sauce
- Two cooked breaded chicken breast strips
- A small amount of thinly sliced lettuce
- Two slices of tomato, diced

Instructions:

1. Microwave the tortilla for 30–45 minutes so that it softens and folds easily.
2. Use mayonnaise sauce to coat the tortilla.
3. Lay the end-to-end chicken tenders on top of the tortilla lengthwise.
4. On top of the chicken, add spinach, onion, and more of the mayonnaise sauce.
5. Fold it like a burrito and savor it.

3.Long John Silver's Beer-Battered Fish

Preparation Time: 40 minutes

Servings: 2 to 4

Difficulty: Moderate

Ingredients:

- Vegetable oil for frying
- One cup McCormick Golden Dipt Beer Batter for Seafood mix
- 2/3 cup beer
- One and a half pounds fish fillets

Instructions:

1. Heat oil to 375 degrees F.
2. Stir the batter and beer mixture in a medium bowl until smooth.
3. Cut into serving-size bits of fish.
4. Dunk fish into batter and shake off any excess.
5. A few bits at a time, slowly add the fish to the hot oil. Cook for 3–5 minutes, turning uniformly once to brown. When it is golden brown and flakes quickly with a fork, the fish is done. Drain the fried fish on paper towels.

4. Sonic Fritos Chili Cheese Wraps

Preparation Time: 35 minutes

Servings: 4

Difficulty: Moderate

Ingredients:

- One (19-ounce) can of mild chili
- Three cups Fritos corn chips
- Four flour tortillas
- One cup shredded mild Cheddar cheese
- A quarter cup of diced green onions

Instructions:

1. Cook the chili on medium-high heat in a shallow saucepan until it bubbles.
2. Remove it from the stove.
3. Combine the chili with the Fritos.
4. Place a quarter of the chili mixture down the center of each tortilla.
5. Sprinkle on top of the chili with a quarter cup of cheese. To taste, add the diced onions. Just fold it into a burrito.
6. To melt the cheese, microwave for 15–20 seconds.

5. Panera Bread Cafe's Sierra Turkey Sandwich

Preparation Time: 2 hours 10 minutes

Servings: 20

Difficulty: Moderate

Ingredients:

- Two and a half C. heavy mayonnaise
- Two Tablespoons sugar
- one-third C. pureed chipotle in adobo sauce
- Three medium limes, juiced
- 20 wedges Asiago cheese focaccia, split
- Five lb. smoked turkey breast, sliced thin
- Two large sweet onions, sliced very thin
- One lb. field greens, washed, dried, and chilled

Instructions:

1. Blend mayonnaise, sugar, pureed chipotle, and lime juice together in a medium bowl. Cover and place in the refrigerator for at least 30 minutes before serving.

2. For Each Serving-On the bottom piece of split focaccia spread, Two tablespoons of chipotle mayonnaise. Top with 4 oz. Turkey and one slice of onion.

3. Lightly cover with greens. Replace top of the focaccia.

6. K.F.C.'s Mac and Cheese

Preparation Time: 40 minutes

Servings: 3

Difficulty: Moderate

Ingredients:

- Six C. water
- One and one-third C. elbow macaroni
- Four oz. Velveeta cheese
- Half C. shredded cheddar cheese
- Two tablespoons s whole milk
- 1/4 teaspoons salt

Instructions:

1. In a medium saucepan, bring water to a boil over high heat. Add the elbow macaroni to the water and cook, occasionally stirring, for 10-12 minutes or until tender.

2. Prepare the cheese sauce when the macaroni is boiling by mixing the remaining ingredients in a shallow saucepan over low heat.

3. When the cheese melts into a smooth consistency, stir sometimes. Strain it and then dump it back into the same pan, without the sauce, when the macaroni is finished. In the pan, add the cheese sauce and stir gently until the cheese is well mixed with the macaroni.

4. While hot, serve immediately.

7. Chick Fillet Chicken Nuggets

Preparation Time: 60 minutes

Servings: 6

Difficulty: Moderate

Ingredients:

- Two Cups Chicken Breast (Boneless, Skinless, Cubed)
- One cup Flour
- One and a half Cups Cracker Meal
- 1/4 teaspoon Paprika
- Two Cups Water
- Two Chicken Bouillon Cubes
- Two and 1/4 teaspoons McCormick Season–all

Instructions:

1. Place cool water in the bowl, add 1/4 teaspoon season–all and dissolve bouillon cubes in the mixture.

2. Place the cubed chicken in the water for 12 hours or the next day, blend, cover and place in the fridge. Combine flour, cracker meal, two teaspoons of season-all and paprika in a cup until preparing to fry nuggets.

3. For deep frying, heat oil. Chicken, drain. Coat the nuggets with flour, combine the crackers, and cook until golden. It'll be flavorful and moist.

8. Hooter's Buffalo Chicken Wings

Preparation Time: 60 minutes

Servings: 6

Difficulty: Moderate

Ingredients:

- 1/4 cup margarine
- 1/4 cup Red Devil Hot Sauce
- 1/4 teaspoon granulated garlic
- Half cup all–purpose flour
- 1/4 teaspoon paprika
- 1/4 teaspoon cayenne pepper
- 1/4 teaspoon salt
- Ten chicken wings, tips removed
- Vegetable oil for frying

Instructions:

1. Heat the oil to 350F in a deep fryer.
2. Melt the margarine and whisk in the garlic and hot sauce. And put aside.
3. In a shallow bowl, combine the flour, paprika, cayenne pepper and salt.
4. In a wide cup, put the wings and spray the flour mixture over them, covering each wing uniformly. Place the wings for 60-90 minutes in the refrigerator. This will allow the breading, when fried, to adhere to the wings.

5. Place all the wings in the hot oil and fry for about 10 minutes or until dark brown. Take it out of the oil and put it in a wide bowl.

6. Add the hot sauce and stir, equally covering all the wings.

7. Serve on the side of blue cheese sauce and pieces of celery.

9. P.F. Chang's Lettuce Wraps

Preparation Time: 60 minutes

Servings: 2 to 4

Difficulty: Moderate

Ingredients:

- Eight dried shiitake mushrooms
- One teaspoon cornstarch
- Two teaspoons dry sherry
- Two teaspoons water
- Salt and pepper
- One and a half pounds boneless, skinless chicken
- Five Tablespoons oil
- One teaspoon fresh minced ginger
- Two cloves garlic, minced
- Two green onions, minced
- Two smalls dried chilis (optional)
- Eight Ounce can bamboo shoots, minced
- Eight Ounce can water chestnuts, minced
- One package of cellophane Chinese rice noodles prepared according to package

Cooking Sauce:

- One tablespoon Hoisin sauce
- One tablespoon soy sauce
- One tablespoon dry sherry

- Two tablespoons of oyster sauce
- Two tablespoons of water
- One teaspoon sesame oil
- One teaspoon sugar
- Two teaspoons cornstarch
- Iceberg lettuce, "cups."

Instructions:

1. Cover with boiling water, let stand for 30 minutes, then drain the mushrooms. Cut the woody stems and discard them. Mince spores. And put aside.

2. In a bowl, combine and set aside all the ingredients for the cooking sauce.

3. Combine the cornstarch, sherry water, soya sauce, salt, pepper, and chicken in a medium bowl. Stir thoroughly to cover the chicken.

4. Stir in one teaspoon of oil and leave to marinate for 15 minutes. Over the medium-high fire, heat the wok or broad skillet. Three tablespoons of oil are added, then the chicken is added and fried for around 3-4 minutes. And put aside.

5. In a pan, heat two tablespoons of oil. Add ginger, garlic, chilies (if desired), and onion; fry for around a minute or so. Add mushrooms, bamboo shoots, chestnuts and water; fry for two more minutes.

6. Put the chicken back in the pan. To the pan, add the blended cooking sauce. Cook until the mixture thickens

and is hot. Break the cooked cellophane noodles into small pieces, shielding them with the bottom of the serving bowl.

7. Then pour the mixture of chicken on top of the noodles.
8. Spoon the leaves into the lettuce and roll.

10. Ruby Tuesday's White Chicken Chili

Preparation Time: 3 hours 10 minutes

Servings: 1

Difficulty: Hard

Ingredients:

- One pound bag of great northern beans (soaked in water overnight)
- Two medium onions, chopped
- Six cups chicken stock
- Six cups diced cooked chicken
- Two jalapeno peppers seeded diced
- Two diced chili peppers
- One and a half teaspoons oregano
- Two teaspoons cumin
- 1/4 teaspoon cayenne pepper
- Two garlic cloves, minced
- One cup of salsa
- One tablespoon vegetable oil
- salt as per taste

Instructions:

1. Simmer the beans, half of both the onions and the garlic in the chicken stock for 2 hours or until the beans are tender, stirring sometimes.

2. Add salsa and chicken. Chili is added to the sauteed peppers, spices, and the remaining onions and garlic in the oil. Simmer for an extra hour.
3. Garnish with whipped cream or Monterey Jack cheese.

Chapter 5: Sauces, Slaws, and Dips Recipes

1. A&W Coney Island Sauce

Preparation Time: 4 hours

Servings: 25 cups

Difficulty: Moderate

Ingredients:

- Sixty-four ounces of Hunt's Tomato Paste
- Sixty -four ounces Hunt's Tomato Purée
- One and a half cups of granulated sugar
- one-third cup of cider vinegar
- Oil
- Two tablespoons of chili powder
- One tablespoon of pepper
- One tablespoon of celery seed
- Three tablespoons and one teaspoon of salt

Instructions:

1. In a saucepan, heat the oil.
2. Add all the ingredients and simmer for three and a half hours.
3. Stir frequently so that the sauce will not stick to the pan.

2. K.F.C. Pepper Mayonnaise Sauce

Preparation Time: 45 minutes

Servings: Half cup

Difficulty: Moderate

Ingredients

- Half cup mayonnaise
- One teaspoon black pepper
- One teaspoon lemon juice

Instructions

1. Combine all of the ingredients with a lid in a shallow bowl.
2. Store in the refrigerator for up to two weeks.

3. Long John Silver's Baja Sauce

Preparation Time: 35 minutes

Servings: 1 and half cup

Difficulty: Moderate

Ingredients

- Half cup sour cream
- Half cup mayonnaise
- Two teaspoons taco seasoning
- One small diced jalapeño pepper
- a quarter cup fresh lime juice
- Half cup chopped fresh cilantro

Instructions

1. Combine all the ingredients with a lid in a shallow tub. Mix thoroughly.
2. Store in the refrigerator for up to 2 weeks.

4. K.F.C. Cole Slaw

Preparation Time: 45 minutes

Servings: 4

Difficulty: Moderate

Ingredients

- One head of cabbage, shredded
- One to two carrots, grated
- 1/4 onion, grated

Dressing:

- 1 C. Miracle Whip Salad Dressing
- 1 C. sugar
- 1/4 C. oil
- 1/4 vinegar

Instructions

1. Mix the dressing and pour over cabbage mix.
2. Let it sit for a few hours before eating.

5. Outback Steakhouse Bloomin' Onion Dipping Sauce

Preparatio Time: 45 minutes

Servings: 4

Difficulty: Moderate

Ingredients

- Half C. mayonnaise
- Two teaspoons ketchup
- Two tablespoons horseradish
- 1/4 teaspoons paprika
- 1/4 teaspoons salt
- 1/8 teaspoons garlic powder
- 1/8 teaspoons dried oregano
- dash ground pepper
- dash cayenne pepper

Instructions

1. Combine all ingredients and mix well.
2. Cover and place in the refrigerator for at least 30 minutes

Chapter 6: Beverages Recipes

1. Jack in the Box's Oreo Cookie Shake

Preparation Time: 15 minutes

Servings: 2

Difficulty: Easy

Ingredients:

- Three cups vanilla ice cream
- One and a half cups milk
- 8 Oreo cookies
- Whipped cream for topping
- Two maraschino cherries for garnish

Instructions:

1. Mix the ice cream and milk in a blender and process until smooth.
2. Break up the cookies and add to the ice cream while the blender is running low. Blend until the cookies are pureed—a few chunks are okay.
3. Pour the blend into two chilled glasses and garnish with whipped cream and a cherry on top.

2. McDonald's Mc Cafe Caramel Cappuccino

Preparation Time: 15 minutes

Servings: 1

Difficulty: Easy

Ingredients:

- Six ounces of strong coffee or two shots of espresso
- Half cup milk
- Two tablespoons caramel ice cream topping, divided use
- Two tablespoons whipped cream garnish

Instructions:

1. Pour in the coffee in a big heated coffee mug.
2. Add one tablespoon caramel syrup to the mixture. Add the warmed milk to it. If needed, fill with whipped cream and then drizzle over the remaining caramel syrup.

3. Starbucks Tazo Chai Tea Latte

Preparation Time: 35 minutes

Servings: 2

Difficulty: Easy

Ingredients:

- Six to eight green cardamom pods
- Two whole black peppercorns
- One or two slices peeled fresh ginger, diced
- Two sticks cinnamon
- One or two whole cloves
- 2/3 cup milk
- Four teaspoons honey
- Two to Three teaspoons loose black tea

Instructions:

1. In a medium saucepan, bring two and a half cups of water to a boil and cardamom, peppercorns, ginger, cinnamon, and cloves. Reduce the heat and simmer for 10 minutes.

2. Stir in the milk and honey. Continue stirring until the honey is dissolved. Bring to a low boil and add the loose tea.

3. Suspend the pan from the heat and let sit for 5 minutes.

4. Strain the solids from the latte and pour into 2 cups. Serve hot.

4. McDonald's Oreo Mc Flurry

Preparation Time: 35 minutes

Servings: 1

Difficulty: Easy

Ingredients:

- Two cups vanilla ice cream
- Two tablespoons whole milk
- Four Oreo cookies

Instructions:

1. Place the ice cream and milk in a mixer and combine the ice cream and milk.

2. Crumble the Oreo cookies into the mixer, press the blender to mix the cookies a couple of times.

3. Drop a drink into it and enjoy it!

5. McDonald's Sweet Tea

Preparation Time: 30 minutes

Servings: 6

Difficulty: Easy

Ingredients:

- Two quarts of water, divided use
- Three family-sized bags of tea or 12 bags of tea
- Two cups of sugar

Instructions:

1. Boil 4 cups (1 quart) of water.
2. Add tea bags and sugar. Stir to mix in the sugar.
3. Reduce the temperature to simmer/low. Steep the tea for five minutes.
4. Fill pitcher full of ice. Pour tea over ice. Add water to the picture to fill the pitcher.
5. Store tea in the refrigerator. You can use less sugar if desired.

6. Chili's Presidente Margarita

Preparation Time: 45 minutes

Servings: 1

Difficulty: Easy

Ingredients:

- One and a quarter ounces Sauza Commemorative Tequila
- Half ounce Presidente Brandy
- Half ounce Cointreau
- 4 ounces sour mix
- Splash of lime juice

Instructions:

1. Mix all ingredients and serve in a salt-rimmed glass filled with ice.

7. McDonald's Mc Cafe Peppermint Mocha

Preparation Time: 35 minutes

Servings: 1

Difficulty: Easy

Ingredients:

- Peppermint Mocha Syrup
- One cup of sugar
- One cup of water
- Two tablespoons cocoa powder
- One teaspoon peppermint extract
- Individual Drink Recipe
- One to two tablespoons peppermint mocha syrup
- One cup of coffee or espresso shot
- One cup milk steamed
- Two tablespoons whipped cream
- One teaspoon chocolate syrup

Instructions:

1. To make the mocha, in a saucepan, mix the sugar and cocoa powder.
2. Afterward, add in the water and bring to a boil, stirring constantly. Remove from heat, add the peppermint extract and allow to cool.
3. Store in an airtight container in the fridge.

4. To make the coffee, Pour the syrup in a coffee mug followed by the coffee.

5. Add the steamed milk.

6. Top it up with whipped cream and chocolate syrup, if desired.

8. McDonald's Eggnog Shake

Preparation Time: 30 minutes

Servings: 1

Difficulty: Easy

Ingredients:

- One cup of vanilla ice cream
- Half cup eggnog
- Two tablespoons whipped cream
- One maraschino cherry

Instructions:

1. Scoop one cup of vanilla ice cream and place that into a blender.
2. Add half a cup of eggnog and pour this into the blender. Puree for about 45 seconds.
3. Pour milkshake into a glass and add whipped cream and a maraschino cherry.

9. Colorado Bulldog Drink

Preparation Time: 20 minutes

Servings: 1

Difficulty: Easy

Ingredients:

- Two ounces Kahlua
- Two ounces Vodka
- One ounce Coca-Cola
- Six ounces of milk, half and half, is preferred.

Instructions:

1. Just use a cocktail shaker to pour Kahlua and vodka over sugar. Just shake good.
2. Add cola and milk. In a bottle, stir and pour.

Conclusion

I'm very glad you've taken the time to read this book.

I hope that with regards to Fast food Copycat Recipes, all your questions are clear.

It is about learning the restaurants' simple ingredients and techniques to make the masterpiece dish to create a Copycat Recipe.

Creating a copy of the popular dish also allows you to adjust the ingredients used according to your tastes and health restrictions to produce a custom recipe.

It is also a cost-effective way to eat popular meals that you want. Keep cooking and try to work with the recipes.

Well, thanks and good luck!

9 781914 129414